6/2018

Hampshire County Public
153 West Main Stree
Romney, WV 26757

D1224276

INSECTS UP CLOSE

Mosquitoes

by Patrick Perish

BLASTOFF! READERS

BELLWETHER MEDIA • MINNEAPOLIS, MN

Note to Librarians, Teachers, and Parents:

Blastoff! Readers are carefully developed by literacy experts and combine standards-based content with developmentally appropriate text.

Level 1 provides the most support through repetition of high-frequency words, light text, predictable sentence patterns, and strong visual support.

Level 2 offers early readers a bit more challenge through varied simple sentences, increased text load, and less repetition of high-frequency words.

Level 3 advances early-fluent readers toward fluency through increased text and concept load, less reliance on visuals, longer sentences, and more literary language.

Level 4 builds reading stamina by providing more text per page, increased use of punctuation, greater variation in sentence patterns, and increasingly challenging vocabulary.

Level 5 encourages children to move from "learning to read" to "reading to learn" by providing even more text, varied writing styles, and less familiar topics.

Whichever book is right for your reader, Blastoff! Readers are the perfect books to build confidence and encourage a love of reading that will last a lifetime!

This edition first published in 2018 by Bellwether Media, Inc.

No part of this publication may be reproduced in whole or in part without written permission of the publisher. For information regarding permission, write to Bellwether Media, Inc., Attention: Permissions Department, 5357 Penn Avenue South, Minneapolis, MN 55419.

Library of Congress Cataloging-in-Publication Data

Names: Perish, Patrick, author.
Title: Mosquitoes / by Patrick Perish.
Description: Minneapolis, MN : Bellwether Media, Inc., 2018. | Series: Blastoff! readers. Insects up close |
    Audience: Age 5-8. | Audience: K to grade 3. | Includes bibliographical references and index.
Identifiers: LCCN 2017028714| ISBN 9781626177178 (hardcover : alk. paper) | ISBN 9781681034102 (ebook)
Subjects: LCSH: Mosquitoes–Juvenile literature.
Classification: LCC QL536 .P442 2018 | DDC 595.77/2-dc23
LC record available at https://lccn.loc.gov/2017028714

Text copyright © 2018 by Bellwether Media, Inc. BLASTOFF! READERS and associated logos are trademarks and/or registered trademarks of Bellwether Media, Inc. SCHOLASTIC, CHILDREN'S PRESS, and associated logos are trademarks and/or registered trademarks of Scholastic Inc., 557 Broadway, New York, NY 10012.

Editor: Nathan Sommer   Designer: Steve Porter

Printed in the United States of America, North Mankato, MN.

Table of **Contents**

What Are Mosquitoes?

A mosquito lands with a quiet hum. This insect sucks blood!

blood

Most mosquitoes are brown or black. Some have stripes or bright colors!

ACTUAL SIZE: southern house mosquito

Mosquitoes only have two wings. Their pointy mouths are like needles.

mouth

wings

9

Mosquito Life

Mosquitoes rest under leaves or in shady holes. Many hide during the day.

Mosquitoes drink **nectar**. Only females suck blood. They need it to make eggs.

FAVORITE FOOD:

nectar

Some mosquitoes
are big pests.
They can spread
diseases.

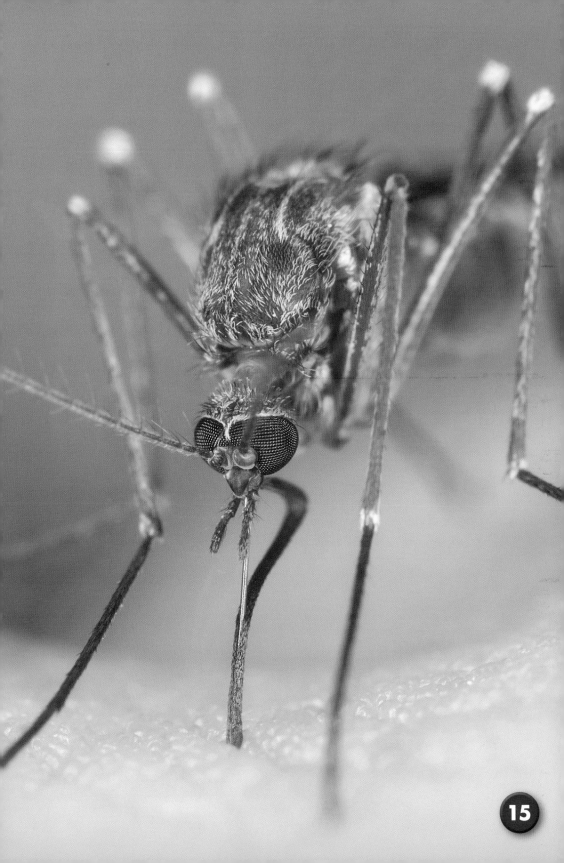

From Water to Air!

Female mosquitoes lay eggs near or on water. **Larvae** soon **hatch**.

larva

FEMALE
MOSQUITO
LIFE SPAN:

about 2 months

Larvae grow in ponds, puddles, and birdbaths! They **molt** to become **pupae**.

pupae

Pupae rest at the water's surface. They open and adult mosquitoes crawl out!

adult mosquito

Glossary

diseases

sicknesses that stop the body from working normally

molt

to shed skin for growth

hatch

to break out of an egg

nectar

a sweet liquid that comes from plants, especially flowers

larvae

baby insects that have come from eggs; larvae look like worms.

pupae

young insects that are about to become adults

To Learn More

AT THE LIBRARY

Carr, Aaron. *Mosquitoes*. New York, N.Y.: AV2 by Weigl, 2016.

Dessen, Maci. *Look Out for the Mosquito!* New York, N.Y.: PowerKids Press, 2015.

Simpson, Caroll. *The First Mosquito*. Victoria, B.C.: Heritage House Publishing, 2015.

ON THE WEB

Learning more about mosquitoes is as easy as 1, 2, 3.

1. Go to www.factsurfer.com.

2. Enter "mosquitoes" into the search box.

3. Click the "Surf" button and you will see a list of related web sites.

With factsurfer.com, finding more information is just a click away.

Index

The images in this book are reproduced through the courtesy of: 7th Son Studio, front cover, pp. 18-19 (pupae), 22 (center left, bottom right); mirceax, pp. 4-5; StevenRussellSmithPhotos, pp. 6-7; Petlia Roman, pp. 6-7 (leaf foreground image); Evgeny Komzolov, p. 7 (mosquito graphic); MR.AUKID PHUMSIRICHAT, pp. 8-9; manode, pp. 10-11; Kerrick, pp. 12-13; Srijira Ruechapaisarnanak, pp. 13 (inset), 22 (center right); Henrik Larsson, pp. 14-15; Amir Ridhwan, pp. 16-17; doug4537, pp. 18-19 (mosquito); hose_bw, pp. 20-21; Sanimfocus, p. 22 (top left); Somporn Pramong, p. 22 (bottom left); Kidsada Manchinda, p. 22 (top right).